Way Ahead

A Foundation Course in English

Pupil's Book **3**

Mary Bowen

Printha Ellis

New Edition

Scope and sequence

All units practise skills in reading, writing, listening and speaking based around particular structures and vocabulary. Specific study skills are listed separately.

Unit	Vocabulary	Study Skills
1 I live in Clifton. Pages 8–12 I go to Woodside School. I get up at six o'clock. In Clifton there is a river.	Personal details; routine Places in a town	Spelling: *ea* Punctuation
2 What is Emma doing? Pages 13–17 The children are learning Science. She's climbing the ladder.	School lessons Adventure playground	Spelling: *oo* Categorising
3 I have two cousins. Pages 18–22 They have a son. Do you have any aunts? His father is a cook. He works in a restaurant.	Family members Jobs and professions	Spelling: 3rd person *s/es* Categorising
4 Let's play in the park. Pages 23–27 I often/sometimes/never play football. Can Ned run across the bridge? Emma doesn't like tennis.	Adverbs of frequency Sport and activities	Spelling: double consonant before *-ing*
5 Birthdays Pages 28–32 When's his birthday? It's on the 15th of May. July is the seventh month.	Ordinals 13th–31st, figures and words	Alphabetical order Capital letters
6 Jill is taller than Emma. Pages 33–37 Sam is heavier. Becky is younger. I weigh 45 kilos. I'm 1 metre 50 centimetres. Are they different? They're the same.	Comparative adjectives Measurements	Spelling: *ow* Finding differences
7 Let's go shopping. Pages 38–42 I'm going to buy a book. Can you see the bakery? Where can I buy shoes? At the shoe shop.	Shops and shopping Alphabetical order	Spelling: *o*
8 We're going to have a picnic. Pages 43–47 Are we going to go to the mountains? They're going to go along the river.	Outings Prepositions of movement	Spelling: *ou* Categorising
9 At the market Pages 48–52 How much is the bread? It's eighty pence. Can I have some eggs, please? Is there any juice?	Food; prices Shopping	Spelling: double letters Long/short forms
10 A picnic Pages 53–57 There are plates and mugs and bowls. Would you like some melon? I'd like some strawberries. Here they are.	Picnic equipment Picnic food	Spelling: rhyming words Identifying syllables

Ned

Emma

Joe

Martin

Jill

Sam

Ben

Lizzie

Becky

1 I live in Clifton.

1 Read and find.

This is Clifton. Can you find a  river and two bridges? Can you point to a school and a playground? Can you see a hill and a castle? Can you find a flower shop and a sweet shop?

2 Listen and read.

Hi! I'm Emma. I live in the new town, too. My flat is near the school. I'm nine.

Hello! My name's Ned. I'm eight. I live in Clifton. I live in the new town near the park. I go to Woodside School.

Hello! My name's Jill and nine. I live in the old tow My house is near the rive

Hi! My name's Sam. I go to Woodside School. I live in a flat in the old town. I'm nine.

Hello! I'm Becky. I'm eight. I live in a house near the sea. I go to Woodside School, too.

Write four sentences about Clifton.

In Clifton there is ...

1 Look at the pictures. This is my day.

A

B

C

D

E

F

2 Read and find.

1 I always get up at seven o' clock. ☐

2 I have breakfast in the kitchen with my family. ☐

3 I go to school at half past eight. I go by car. ☐

4 I come home at half past three. I always watch TV and play with my toys. ☐

5 In the evening I do my homework. ☐

6 At half past nine I say 'Goodnight' to my mother and my father and I go to bed. ☐

3 Write.

Write three sentences about your day.

1 **Look and read.**

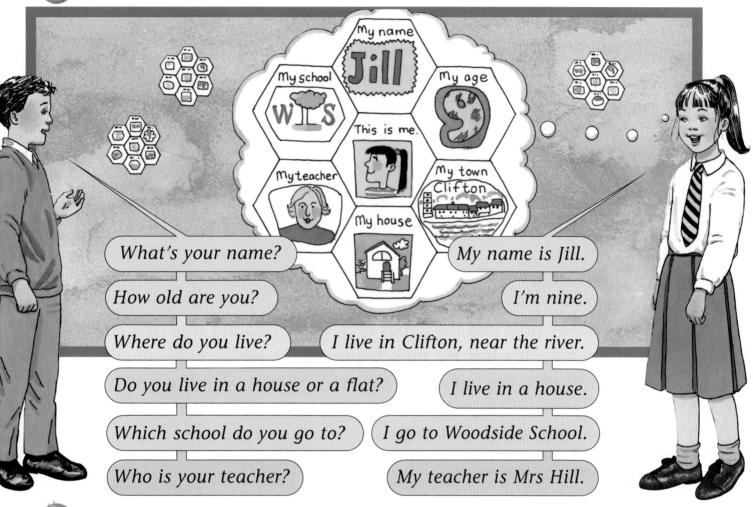

What's your name? My name is Jill.

How old are you? I'm nine.

Where do you live? I live in Clifton, near the river.

Do you live in a house or a flat? I live in a house.

Which school do you go to? I go to Woodside School.

Who is your teacher? My teacher is Mrs Hill.

2 **Now you!**

3 **Listen and sing.**

The sun wakes up,
Yes, the sun wakes up.

The sun smiles,
Yes, the sun smiles.

The wind blows,
Yes, the wind blows.

The rain falls down,
Yes, the rain falls down.

The sun goes down,
Yes, the sun goes down.

The moon comes up,
Yes, the moon comes up.

The night lies still,
Yes, the night lies still.

Then the sun wakes up,
Yes, the sun wakes up.

The circus monkey

The music is playing. The lights are shining.
The children are laughing and talking.

The monkey runs into the circus ring. He is wearing a purple jacket
and a funny little hat. He runs, he jumps, he walks on his hands.
He stands on a big ball and holds an umbrella. He rides a
pink bicycle and plays a golden trumpet. He waves to the
children. They laugh and clap.

At night he looks through the bars of his cage and
sees the moon. He shuts his eyes and sleeps.

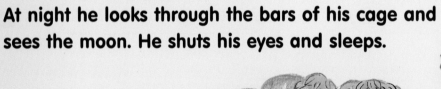

He sees a forest, dark and green. He feels warm
rain on his face. He hears a parrot, a snake, a tiger.
He swings and swings and swings through the trees.

2 What is Emma doing?

1 Listen, read and find.

What is Emma doing? What is Joe doing? What is on the floor?

2 Point, ask and answer.

1 Read and say.

Emma's mother is a teacher.
She's writing the date.
What's the time?

The children are learning Maths.
Jill's doing a sum.
What's the time?

The children are learning English.
The teacher is reading a story.
Ned isn't listening. He's talking to Sam.
What's the time?

The children are doing Art.
Becky's painting a picture.
What's the time?

The children are learning Science.
Jill's watching a video. Ned and
Sam aren't watching. They're talking.
What's the time?

The children are doing Music.
Ned is playing the guitar and Sam is singing.
What's the time?

2 Ask and answer.

The children are doing Art.
What's the time?

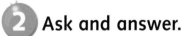

She's watching a video.
Who is it?

It's quarter past one.

It's Jill.

1 **Look at this!**

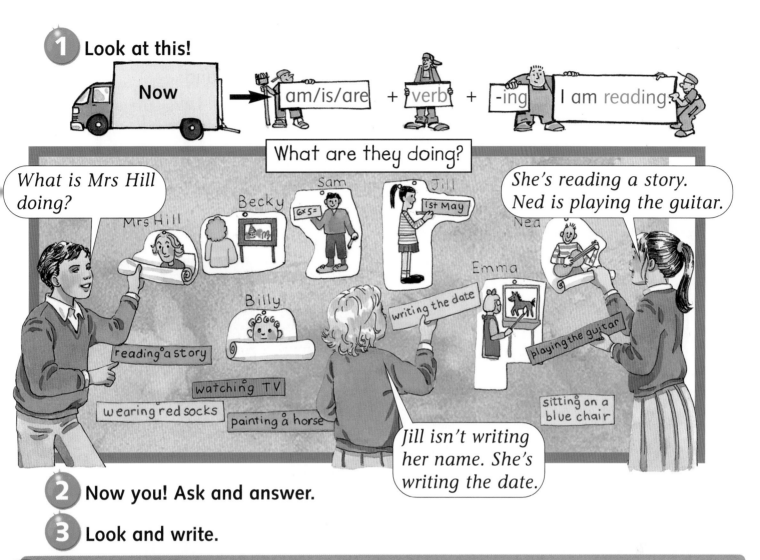

Now → am/is/are + verb + -ing   I am reading.

What are they doing?

What is Mrs Hill doing?

She's reading a story.
Ned is playing the guitar.

Mrs Hill — reading a story

Becky

Sam — 6×5=

watching TV

Billy

wearing red socks   painting a horse

Jill — 1st May — writing the date

Emma

Ned — playing the guitar

sitting on a blue chair

Jill isn't writing her name. She's writing the date.

2 **Now you! Ask and answer.**

3 **Look and write.**

Find these children in your class. Write the names.

_____ is sitting next to the window.

_____ is wearing brown shoes.

_____ and _____ are sitting at the front.

_____ and _____ are wearing glasses.

_____ is sitting at the back.

_____ is wearing a big watch.

4 **Ask and answer.**

She's wearing brown shoes. Who is it?

They're wearing glasses. Who are they?

Write about two children in your class. Where are they sitting? What are they wearing?

1 Look at the pictures.

Andy and Mary are playing in an adventure playground.

Can you find a ladder , a bridge ,

a slide  and a ship  ?

2 Listen, draw and write numbers.

3 Read and find. Write the numbers.

They're in the playground. ☐   He's on the bridge. ☐

They're on the slide. ☐   They're next to the ship. ☐

She's climbing the ladder. ☐   He's looking up at the bridge. ☐

A new school

Outside ...

Here is the digger. It is digging.

Here is the lorry.
It is carrying the bricks.

Here is the cement mixer.
It is making cement.

... and inside ...

Here are the plumbers.
They are putting in pipes.

Here are the windows and
there are the doors.

Here are the carpenters.
They are making the floors.

And here are the children. They're laughing and singing,
they're reading and writing, they're running and swinging.

3 I have two cousins.

1 Listen and read.

My Uncle David has a boat. He loves his boat. Aunt Lily doesn't like the boat.

My uncle and aunt have two children. They have a daughter called Jill and a son called Martin. They are my cousins.

They like their father's boat.

And we like it too!

2 Find.

 her uncle   their son   his cousins   her aunt   their daughter   her cousins

3 Ask and answer.

Do you have any brothers?

Do you have any sisters?

Yes, I have two brothers.

No, I don't have any sisters.

brothers   sisters   uncles   aunts   cousins

1 **Look and say.**

reporter   housewife   policeman   teacher   dentist   artist

2 **Read and answer.**

Emma's father is a policeman. He works in the old town.
He is working now. He is talking to a young man.

What does he do? Where does he work?
Is he working now? What is he doing?

Emma's mother is a teacher. She teaches Maths.
She isn't teaching now. She's having a cup of tea.

What does she do? What does she teach?
Is she teaching now? What is she doing?

3 **Ask and answer.**

1 Look and read.

Firemen

What do firemen do?

They put out fires with a hose.

They help people.

They help animals, too.

What do firemen wear?

They wear jackets, trousers, big boots and yellow helmets.

1 This is John.
He is a fireman.

2 John drives the fire engine but he isn't driving it now. He is cleaning it.

3 The alarm bell is ringing. There is a fire in a shop in the town.

4 The firemen are putting on their jackets and helmets. They are running to the fire engine.

5 Look at John! He is driving very fast to the fire.

2 True or false?

Firemen put out fires.
Firemen wear red helmets.
John drives a van.
John drives a fire engine.

3 Find the right picture.

John is cleaning the fire engine.
John is driving the fire engine.
The bell is ringing.
John is wearing his helmet.

4 Name these things.

1 Look at this!

Present simple

| verb | She plays. |

Present continuous

| am/is/are | + verb | + -ing | She is playing. |

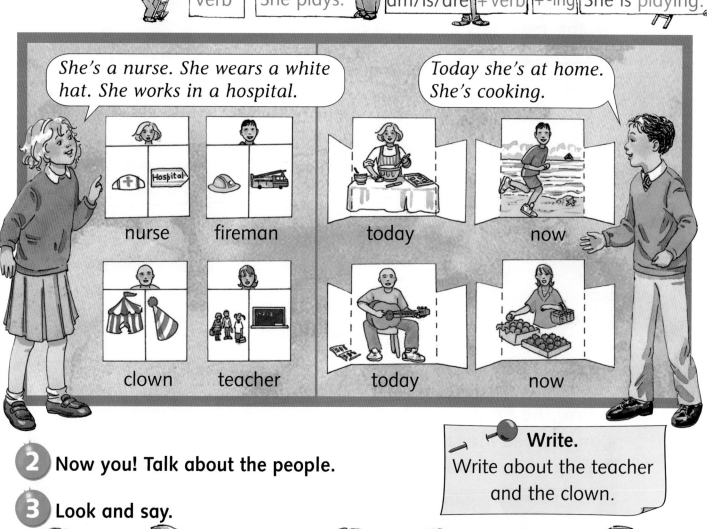

She's a nurse. She wears a white hat. She works in a hospital.

Today she's at home. She's cooking.

nurse fireman

clown teacher

today now

today now

2 Now you! Talk about the people.

Write.
Write about the teacher and the clown.

3 Look and say.

 doctor   farmer   carpenter   cook   waiter   fireman   reporter

1 2 3 4 5 6

7 8 9 10 11 12

Whose is this? *It's the carpenter's.*

NIGHT WORKERS

At night you are sleeping in your warm bed.
In the town lots of people are working.

The baker is making bread for
your breakfast. Look! He is putting
the bread into the hot oven.

An ambulance is taking a boy
to hospital. The boy is ill.

At the hospital the doctors
and nurses are busy.

Firemen are driving quickly to
a fire. The fire is in a shop.
Can you see the shopkeeper?
A policeman is helping him.

In an office a reporter is writing
a story. The telephone rings.
'Come quickly!' a man says.
'There is a fire in Mr Kay's shop.'

A taxi driver is driving his taxi.
A street cleaner is cleaning
the street.

Lots of people are working. And
you are sleeping in your warm bed.

4 Let's play in the park.

1 **Listen and read.**

Let's go and play in the park! Follow me!

Can you find these in the park?

slide   puddle   fence   bridge   swing

I can slide down this big slide. Can you?

Yes, I can. Look!

Oops!

I can run across this bridge. Can you?

No, I can't!

I can jump over this fence.

So can I!

Oops!

Wheeee! Look at me! I can swing across this puddle!

Oh no, you can't!

Oops!

2 **Ask and answer.**

Can Ned run across the bridge?

Yes, he can.

Can Sam?

No, he can't.

1 Read and match.

I like computer games and I like fishing. I never play football. I don't like it.

I like sports. I like football and basketball. I often play football after school.

I like sports. I often play tennis. Sometimes I swim in the sea.

I don't like sports. I never swim or play tennis. I like reading books and I often play computer games.

I like basketball. I don't like fishing but I like swimming in the swimming pool.

2 Read and ✔ or ✗.

	🏊	🐟	⚽	🏀	🎾	💻
Emma	✗				✗	✔
Sam						
Becky						
Ned						
Jill						

3 Look and say.

 Emma doesn't like swimming.

She likes computer games.

1 **Look at this.**

2 **Write your name, look and say.**

Emma never plays tennis.
I sometimes play tennis.

3 **Listen and say.**

I'm making a list of things I like doing.

Swimming and splashing and
Running and leaping,
Whistling and singing and
Eating and sleeping.
Having a picnic,
Climbing a tree.
Reading a good book,
Watching TV.

Write.
Make a list.
I like ... and ...

1 **Listen and say.**

A

roller skates

B
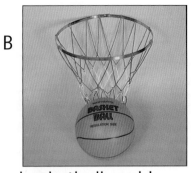
basketball and hoop

C

mountain bike and helmet

D

guitar and drums

E

computer (with twenty games)

F
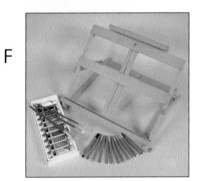
paints and coloured pencils

1  ☐
2 ☐
3 ☐
4 ☐
5  ☐
6  ☐

2 **Choose and say.**

I like ...

I often play ...

I don't have a ...

I like this ...

I like these ...

The Birthday

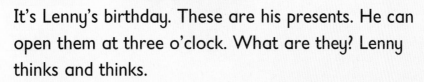

It's Lenny's birthday. These are his presents. He can open them at three o'clock. What are they? Lenny thinks and thinks.

He looks at the blue present.

'This is big,' he thinks. 'Is it a bike? I don't have a bike.'

'What's this red present?' Lenny's cat, Bobbin, comes into the room. She looks at the red present. She sniffs. 'Maybe it's sweets,' Lenny thinks. 'Chocolates!'

Bobbin jumps on the green present. It falls on the floor. 'Oops,' says Lenny. 'Brrrrrrrrrrrrrrrrring,' goes the present. It doesn't stop.

'Is it a clock?' thinks Lenny. 'I don't like clocks!'

Lenny picks up the yellow present. 'What's this yellow one? Is it a T-shirt? A football shirt?'

He hears the grandfather clock, 'Bong! Bong! Bong!' Three o'clock!

The door opens. Here are his friends! It's a party!

'Happy Birthday, Lenny,' his friends say.

Now Lenny can open his presents. Is he right?

5 Birthdays

1 Read and say.

July.

July is the seventh month.

2 A game.

Is it June?

No, it isn't.

Is it before June?

No, it isn't.

Is it after August?

Yes, it is.

Is it September?

Yes, it is.

3 Listen and sing.

There are twelve months in a year.
There are twelve months in a year.
From January to December
There are twelve months in a year.

It's the fourth month.
It's the fourth month.
It's the fourth month in the year.

It's April!
It's April!
It's the fourth month in the year.

1 Listen and read.

It's Mrs Hill's birthday on the 13ᵗʰ of March.

Happy Birthday to you!

Thank you, children. It's very kind of you. But my birthday is on the 30ᵗʰ of March, not the 13ᵗʰ!

Sorry!

2 Look at this!

MAY
1 2 3 4 5 6 7
8 9 10 11 12 13 14
15 16 17 18 19 20 21
22 23 24 25 26 27 28
29 30 31

AUGUST
1 2 3 4 5 6 7
8 9 10 11 12 13 14
15 16 17 18 19 20 21
22 23 24 25 26 27 28
29 30 31

DECEMBER
1 2 3 4 5 6 7
8 9 10 11 12 13 14
15 16 17 18 19 20 21
22 23 24 25 26 27 28
29 30 31

Ned   Emma   Joe   Jill   Becky   Sam

3 Read and write.

His birthday is on the 15ᵗʰ of May. Who is it? _____

Her birthday is on the 22ⁿᵈ of August. Who is it? _____

His birthday is on the 31ˢᵗ of December. Who is it? _____

4 Ask and answer.

When's his birthday?

It's on the 15ᵗʰ of May.

When's your birthday?

1 Look and say.

His name's … Her name's … He's … She's … They live in … They go to …	always get up brush teeth

always go to school ride/bike come home	like art can paint has	like music can sing has

2 Listen and sing.

I am a music man,
I come from far away,
And I can play …   What can you play?

I play the piano.	I play the big drum.	I play the trumpet.
Pi-a, pi-a, piano,	Boom-di, boom-di, boom-di-boom,	Toot-ti, toot-ti, toot-ti-to
Piano, piano,	Boom-di-boom, boom-di-boom,	Toot-ti-toot, toot-ti-toot,
Pi-a, pi-a, piano,	Boom-di, boom-di, boom-di-boom,	Toot-ti, toot-ti, toot-ti-to
Pi-a, piano.	Boom-di-boom-di-boom.	Toot-ti, toot-ti-toot.

Write four sentences
about Becky or Ned.

1 **Ask and answer. Use the words in the shapes.**

Where is the fireman going?

down   into   across   over   onto   up   under

Is he going under the wall?

No, he isn't.

Is he going over the wall?

Yes, he is.

2 **Listen and check.**

3 **Match and say.**   What does number 1 do?   He's a policeman.

housewife   policeman   artist   reporter   dentist

1   2   3   4   5

4 **Look and say.**

What are they doing in the picture?   The policeman is watching TV.

I want to be ...

I want to be a sailor.

I want to drive a train.

I want to be a pilot and fly an aeroplane.

I want to be a fireman.

I want to be a clown.

I want to be a cook - the best in the town.

I want to be a farmer.

I want to drive fast cars.

I want to be a spaceman and travel to the stars.

My Sunday Socks

Monday morning I put rocks in my socks.

Tuesday morning I put my socks in a box.

Wednesday morning I put the box on a goat.

Thursday morning I put the goat in coat.

Friday morning I put the coat in a tree.

Saturday morning I put the tree in the sea.

Sunday morning I put the socks on me!

Dr Fitzhugh Dodson

6 Jill is taller than Emma.

1 **Look and say. Are they the same? Are they different?**

2 **Listen, read and ✔.**

How much do you weigh?

I weigh 45 kilos.

I weigh 38 kilos.

How tall are you?

I'm 1 metre 50 centimetres.

I'm 1 metre 36 centimetres.

	Sam	Ned
Who is heavier?	✔	
Who is lighter?		✔

	Jill	Emma
Who is taller?		
Who is shorter?		

How old are you?

I'm eight.

I'm nine.

	cky	Jill
Who is older?		
Who is younger?		

Show me your hands.

This is my hand.

This is my hand.

	Sam's	Emma's
Which hand is bigger?		
Which hand is smaller?		

Write. ➞ ➞●
Answer the questions
under the pictures,
like this: Sam is heavier.

Comparison   Unit 6   Lesson 1

1 Look and find.

Can you see the  school? The castle? Ned's building? Sam's building? The red bridge? The black bridge? Jill's house? Becky's house?

2 Read and say.

Clifton is near the sea.

The new town is smaller than the old town.

There is a river between the old town and the new town.

The red bridge is older than the black bridge.

Jill's house is bigger than Becky's house.

The castle is older than the school.

Sam's building is taller than Ned's building.

Yes, that's right.

No, that's wrong.
The new town is bigger.

1 **Look at this!**

different and the same

adjective + er + than

Joe is taller than Jim.

Joe   Jim   Pat   Pam   Kay   Fay   Len   Ken

Len is shorter than Ken.
Kay and Ken are the same.

2 **Talk about the people. Write about the people.**

3 **Measure and say.**

No. Kay is taller.

Is Len taller than Kay?

4 **Look and say. Measure and say.**

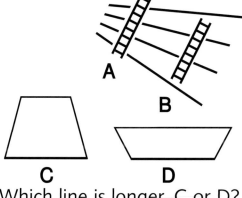

A

B

C   D

Which line is longer, C or D?

G

H

Which boy is taller, G or H?

I think A is longer than B.

No. They're the same!

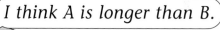

E   F

Which line is shorter, E or F?

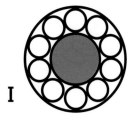
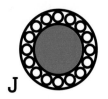

I   J

Which red circle is smaller, I or J?

1 **Look and listen.**

2 **Read and match.**

Be careful!
Drive slowly! ☐

Come on, Roy!
Come here! ☐

Speak quietly! ☐

Speak loudly! ☐

Don't run! ☐

Don't play
football here! ☐

3 **Now you!**

Run quickly!

Clap slowly!

Sing quietly!

Ha! Ha! Ha!

Laugh loudly!

Imperatives; adverbs

Who is strong?

Kay is little. She has a big brother, Ben. Ben is strong.

He can lift a bike – with one hand!

'I am strong too,' says Kay. 'No you're not,' says Ben. 'You're not strong like me.'

'Look,' says Kay, 'put your fists together, like this. Can you keep them together?' 'Yes, I can,' says Ben.

'I can separate your fists,' says Kay. 'No, you can't,' says Ben.

'Yes, I can,' says Kay. Ben pushes his fists together.

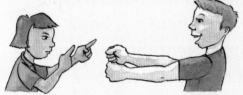

'Watch this,' says Kay. She has her fingers ready. Ben laughs.

With her fingers, Kay knocks Ben's fists sideways.

'Oh!' says Ben.

'See! I am strong after all!' says Kay.

You can do this trick too. Try it on someone strong!

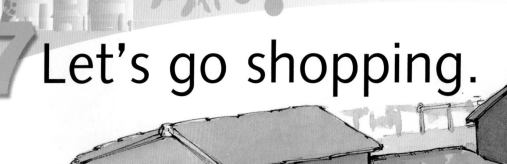

Let's go shopping.

1 Read and find.

There are many shops in Clifton. Can you find the bakery? You can see a shoe shop next to the bakery. And there is a book shop between the bakery and the toy shop. Near the toy shop there is a sports shop and a bike shop. And next to the bike shop there is a sweet shop. And can you see the flower shop?

2 Ask and answer.

Where can I buy shoes? *At the shoe shop.*

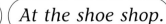

shoes   chocolates   books   biscuits and cakes   football shirts and skates   games   bikes

3 Look and say.

I can buy boots here. Where am I?   *You're in the shoe shop!*

1 Listen and read.

It's Saturday and the children are going shopping. What are they going to buy?

My mother's going to buy some new shoes and I'm going to buy a new book!

I'm going to buy some football boots! My father's going to buy a new bike.

My mother's going to buy some nice cakes and I'm going to buy a book.

I'm going to buy some sweets and a new computer game.

I'm going to buy some flowers and some chocolates for my Aunt Lily.

2 Look and say.

What are Jill and her mother going to buy?
Where are they going to go?

Write three sentences.
Jill's going to buy ...
and her mother's
going to buy ...

1 **Look at the pictures.**

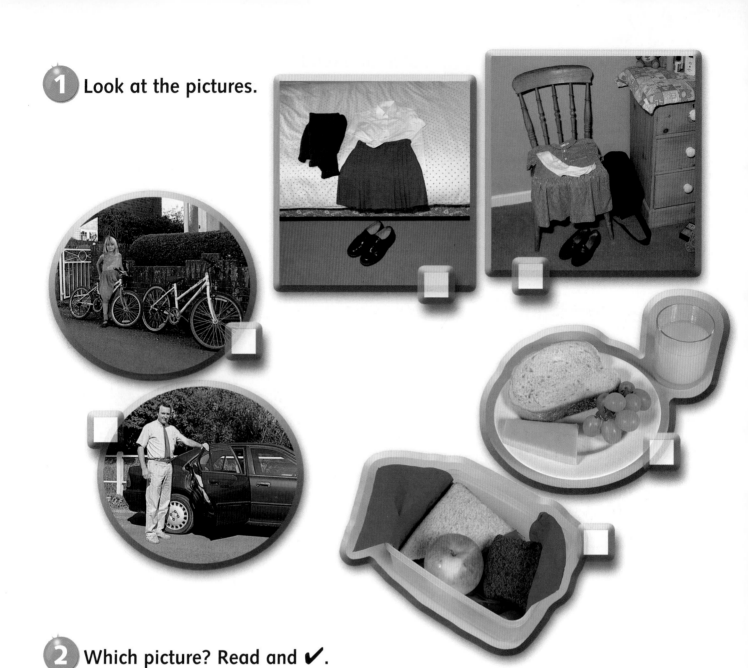

2 **Which picture? Read and ✔.**

It's Monday morning. Jenny is going to go to school at 8 o'clock. She's going to wear a blue and white dress, black shoes and white socks.

Is she going to go to school by car? No, she isn't. She and her friend are going to ride their bikes.

What is she going to have for lunch? She's going to have a sandwich, an apple – and chocolate cake!

3 **Write.**

Write two things Jenny is going to do. Then write one thing she isn't going to do.

1 **Look at this!**

future

to be + going to + verb | I am going to watch TV.

Things we are going to do after school.

We are going to ride our bikes.

read a

Emma | Billy

watch

Ned | Becky

have a

help

Jill | Sam

ride

Ned | Billy

do

Jill | Emma

play with

Jill | Molly | Sam

go to

Becky

They are going to play with friends. What are you going to do?

I'm going to do homework.

I'm not going to go to bed. I'm going to help my mother.

2 **Ask and answer.**

Are you going to ride a bike?

Are you going to watch TV?

Yes, I am.

No, I'm not.

3 **Play a shopping game.**

I'm going to buy something beginning with 'd'.

Are you going to buy a ?

No, I'm not.

Are you going to buy a ?

Yes, I am.

The supermarket

I'm going to the supermarket with my mum. I like the supermarket. You can buy lots of things there.

Look at the fruit! There are apples and bananas, and melons and grapes. Mum is going to buy some strawberries. I love strawberries!

Here are the vegetables. I can see potatoes and peas and carrots.

Mum is looking at the bakery. Is she going to buy any cakes? No, she isn't. But she's going to buy some chocolate biscuits. Yummy!

Here are some toys. 'Mum! Are we going to buy any toys?' Not today!

Hmmmm! What is she looking at now? Magazines. And she's going to buy me a colouring book.

Here's Mr Goody. This is his shop. Mrs Goody is his wife. She always gives me a sweet. 'Here you are, Billy,' she says. 'Thank you, Mrs Goody,' I say.`

I really like Mr Goody's supermarket!

8 We're going to have a picnic.

1 Listen and read.

Dear Becky,
Please come to my house at 11 o'clock on Saturday.
From, Jill.

Can you come?

Yes, I can.

What are we going to do?

We're going to have a picnic.

Where?

Are we going to go to the beach?

No.

Are we going to go to the mountains?

No, we aren't.

Where are we going to have the picnic?

On Rocky Island!

Dad's going to take us on his boat!

Wow!

Fantastic!

2 Read and say.

The children are going to have a party.

No, they aren't. They're going to have a picnic.

They're going to have it on Sunday.

They're going to go to the beach.

Jill's mother is going to take them.

They're going to go by car.

Write
What are the children going to do? Write four sentences.

1 **Look and listen.**

Come and look at the map!

First we're going to go under the bridges …

… and past the castle.

Then we're going to go along the river.

Look! Here's Rocky Island. We're going to go round the island …

… and stop at Rocky Beach. We can go onto the island here and have our picnic.

2 **Put the pictures in the right order.**

3 **Speak.**

First they're going to …

Then they're going to …

Planning; prepositions (movement)

1 **Look at this!**

The cat is going to go …

along the wall, … onto the chair, … round the dog … and past the mouse.

2 **Read, draw and say.**

under   round   past   onto   along   through   into

3 **Read and look.**

On Saturday Jill is going to have a picnic with her friends.

They're going to go by boat to Rocky Island. What are they going to wear? What are they going to take?

Who is going to wear jeans? Who is going to take sunglasses?

Who is going to wear a pullover? Who is going to take a bag?

Emma	Sam	Becky	Ned
Wear:	Wear:	Wear:	Wear:
Take:	Take:	Take:	Take:

4 **Ask and answer.**

What's Becky going to wear?   She's going to wear a …

What's Ned going to take?   He's going to take a …

1 Look, listen and draw lines.

Look at the photos of Judy. She is going home from school. Listen and find the first photo. Listen and draw a line to the next photo.

2 Listen again and number the photos.

3 Speak.

Judy is going past the flower shop.

That's number three.

Clever Max

"Sorry, Max. You can't come with us."

Mike and Lisa are going to visit their grandmother. It is her birthday today. They have cards and balloons. Mum is carrying a birthday cake. Dad is carrying a present. They are going to go to Grandma's house by car. Max, their dog, cannot go to Grandma's house with them. The car is very small.

Dad opens the car.

They all get inside.

And off they go!

"Where's the present?"

"I don't know."

"Woof! Woof!"

Here they are at Grandma's house. She likes the cards and the balloons. She likes the cake, too. She is very happy. But where is her present?

"It's Max!"

"You are a clever dog, Max!"

Max has Grandma's present.

"Thank you very much. It's a lovely pullover."

"Thank you, Max."

Grandma's present is a new pullover. She likes it very much. The family is very happy. And Max is happy, too.

9 At the market

We're going to have a picnic. Here's the shopping list. Are these things in the market?

Shopping List
- eggs ___
- strawberries ___
- cheese ___
- lettuce ___
- orange juice ___
- tomatoes ___
- bread ___
- melons ___
- ice cream ___

1 Read, find and ✔.

carrots
peas
potatoes
fish
lettuce
tomatoes
bananas
apples
oranges
melons
eggs
strawberries

2 Look and say.

Are there any strawberries?

Yes, there are some strawberries.

Is there any bread?

No, there isn't any bread.

3 Spelling.

Write three words for food on cards. Work in teams.

Spell eggs.

eggs

e g g s

1 **Listen and say.**
Who is it?

Excuse me, can I have some cheese?

Excuse me, where's the orange juice?

Can I have some ice cream, please?

Can I have some bread, please?

2 **Look and say.**

Bread is twenty-seven pence.

19p 27p 36p 42p 51p 63p 78p 84p 95p

3 **Ask and answer.**

How much is ice cream?

It's forty-two pence.

How much are oranges?

They're fifty-one pence.

1 **Look and read.**

You can buy these in the supermarket.

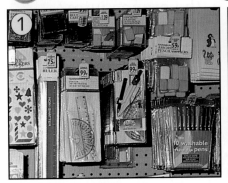

1

These are for school. Can you see what they are?

2

Do you like juice? What fruits can you see?

3

I like the pink cakes and the chocolate biscuits. What do you like?

4

These are sweets. They are many colours. How many colours are there?

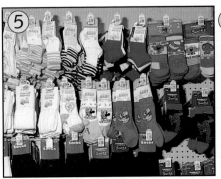

5

Look! Children's socks. Do you like the boys' socks or the girls' socks?

6

Ooh! Lots of ice cream. I like vanilla. Do you?

2 **Read and match.**

I'm going to buy a ruler, a notebook and some paints. ☐

I'm going to buy the pink socks. They're girls' socks. ☐

The chocolate cake is nicer than the white cake. ☐

I like apple juice. Grape juice is nice, too. ☐

I'm going to buy some red and white sweets. ☐

I like strawberry ice cream. ☐

3 **Ask and answer.**

Where's the ruler?

It's in the first picture.

Choose six things. Then write. I am going to buy ... and ...

1 Look at this!

is ... are ... +
some ... any ...

bread   butter   milk

There is + some ...
Is there + any ...?
There is + not + any ...

apples   eggs   carrots

There are + some ...
Are there + some ...?
There are + not + any ...

2 Ask and answer.

Excuse me. Is there any apple juice, please?

No, there isn't any apple juice.

Are there any melons?

Yes, there are some melons.

Shopping List
apple juice
melons
cheese
milk   peas
eggs   carrots
butter bread
strawberries

cheese   melons   peas   bread   eggs   butter   carrots

3 Listen and sing.

I-tiddly-i-ti,
Eat brown bread.
I see a chicken –
It falls down dead.
Up jumps a banana
And bops it on the head.
I-tiddly-i-ti,
– BROWN BREAD!

Ice cream

These words are from a song. Can you say them? Can you scream them?

" I scream, you scream,
      We all scream for ice cream! "

Do you like ice cream? You can make this yummy ice cream sundae.
Ask your mother.

Shopping list

ice cream
bananas
strawberries
chocolate
nuts
cream

Find in the kitchen

plate

knife

spoons

pan

bowl

1 Peel the banana.
➡ 2 Cut it in two.

3 Put it on the plate.
4 Put the chocolate in a bowl.

5 Put the bowl on a pan of hot water.
➡ 6 Melt the chocolate.

7 Put the ice cream on the banana.
8 Put the chocolate on the ice cream.

9 Put the nuts, strawberries and cream on top.

10 Eat your sundae quickly!

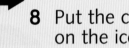
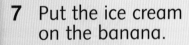

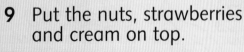

Yum!

Yum!

10 A picnic

1 Listen and read.

We're on Dad's boat. We're going to go to the island and we're going to have a picnic.

What's in the basket?

There are plates and mugs and bowls.

And spoons and forks and a knife.

It's a picnic basket. Look!

Where is the food?

Oh no! Look at this.

Is it a mouse?

No! It's a big bird. There it is! Over there!

Here it is! In the ice box.

This is my pet seagull, Suki. She lives on the boat!

Look! There's the island.

Let's go! I'm hungry.

So are we!

2 Look and find the names.

3 Look and say.

Yes, that's right.

No, that's wrong. The food is in the ice box.

Dad has a pet bird.

The food is in the picnic basket.

There are five spoons and forks.

Suki lives on the island.

Ned can see the island.

Emma has a picnic basket.

1 Listen and sing.

We're going on a picnic,
Leaving right away.
We are going to stay all day.
Would you like some ice cream?
Yes, we'd like some ice cream.
Would you like some salad?
Yes, we'd like some salad.
Ready for a picnic.
Here we go!

Menu
lettuce and tomato salad
cheese or egg sandwiches
melon
strawberries and ice cream
orange juice

Would you like some melon?
Would you like some sandwiches?
Would you like some orange juice?
Would you like some strawberries?

2 Listen and number.

1 Would you like some sandwiches?

Yes, please. ☐

2 Would you like some melon?

Yes, I'd like some sandwiches. ☐

3 I'd like some strawberries.

I have the orange juice. ☐

4 Where's the orange juice?

No, thank you. ☐

5 Would you like some ice cream?

Here's the salad. ☐

6 I'd like some lettuce and tomatoes.

Here they are. ☐

3 Point, ask and answer.

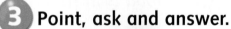

Would you like some ... ?

Yes, please.   No, thank you.

1 Look and read.

What are we going to do now?

Are we going to go swimming?

Are we going to play football?

We're going to see ...

What are we going to see?

2 Ask and answer.

animals	birds	a castle	waterfall	cave	a lighthouse
✗	✗	✓	✗	✓	✗

Are they going to see animals?

No, they aren't.

3 Read and match. Write the letters.

A	B	C	D	E
Speak quietly!	Be careful!	Come here!	Look at this!	Don't run!

1 **Look and say.**

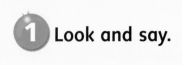

Jill is taller.

2 **Read and say.**

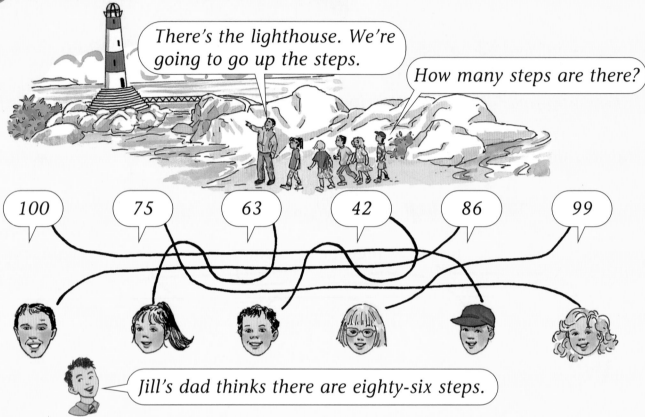

There's the lighthouse. We're going to go up the steps.

How many steps are there?

| 100 | 75 | 63 | 42 | 86 | 99 |

Jill's dad thinks there are eighty-six steps.

3 **Listen and write.**

How many steps are there?_____ Who is right?_____

4 **Talk about the picture.**

Write
What are they doing? Write four sentences about the picture.

Buildings

Buildings are a great suprise,
Every one's a different size.

Offices
grow
tall
and
high,
tall
enough
to
touch
the
sky.

Houses seem
more like a box
made of glue
and building blocks.

Every time you look, you see
Buildings shaped quite differently.

11 He was a very pretty baby.

1 **Look and read.**

Look at this photo! Who is it?

It's me! I was two.

You're thin now but you were very fat! Your hair was blonde and curly! You were very pretty.

Thanks!

2 **Listen and say.**

Becky

Ned

Emma

Sam

3 **Listen and read.**

He was a very pretty baby.
His eyes were big and brown.
His nose was small. His mouth was small.
His ears were small and his hands were small.
And his little pink feet – so sweet!
Yes, he was a very pretty baby.

But – oh dear! – look at him now …

Write.
Write about Becky, Ned, Emma or Sam. Like this: Becky was …
Her hair was …

1 **Look, listen and read.**

2 **Look and speak.**

1 **Look and find.**

Can you see …

a  bench? water?  ducks? a  wet dog?

2 **Read and ✔ picture A or picture B.**

A ☐

B ☐

Yesterday was Saturday. Billy was not at school. It was a nice, sunny day. Billy and his friends were in the park. A big dog was in the park, too. It was black and white with a long tail. It was a nice dog.

A ☐

B ☐

Where was Billy's ball? Was it in the tree? Was it under the bench? Was it in the flowers? No, it was not in the tree or under the bench or in the flowers. It was in the pond!

A ☐

B ☐

Splash! The dog was in the water. The ducks were not happy. Billy and his friends were not happy. The dog was very happy and very wet.

Look at that bad dog!
Come back! Come back, you naughty dog!

3 **Write.**

Write two things about Billy. Billy was …
Write two things about the dog. The dog was …

1 **Look at this!**

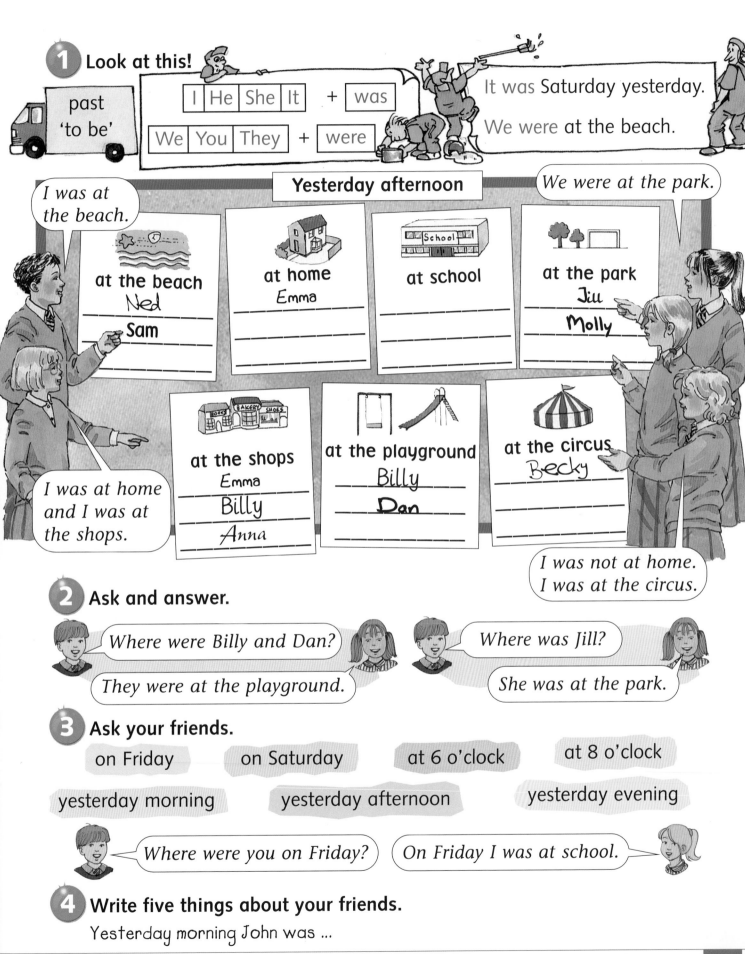

| I | He | She | It | + | was |

| We | You | They | + | were |

It was Saturday yesterday.

We were at the beach.

Yesterday afternoon

I was at the beach.

We were at the park.

at the beach
Ned
Sam

at home
Emma

at school

at the park
Jill
Molly

I was at home and I was at the shops.

at the shops
Emma
Billy
Anna

at the playground
Billy
Dan

at the circus
Becky

I was not at home. I was at the circus.

2 **Ask and answer.**

Where were Billy and Dan?

They were at the playground.

Where was Jill?

She was at the park.

3 **Ask your friends.**

on Friday   on Saturday   at 6 o'clock   at 8 o'clock

yesterday morning   yesterday afternoon   yesterday evening

Where were you on Friday?   *On Friday I was at school.*

4 **Write five things about your friends.**

Yesterday morning John was ...

What is it? Can you guess?

'What do you have under that cloth?' asked the children.
'A very beautiful creature, ' said the teacher. 'Can you guess?'
'Is it a bird?'
'No.'
'Is it a fish?'
'No.'
'Is it a snake?'
'A snake? No, it isn't.'

'Once upon a time this creature was a little, round, brown egg. The egg was on a leaf and the leaf was on a flower in a big field. Can you guess? No?'

'Inside the egg was a caterpillar. It was green and black and gold. It liked the leaves on the flowers in the big field. Mmmm! They were delicious! The caterpillar got bigger and bigger, fatter and fatter.'

'Then one day the caterpillar wasn't there. Where was it? On one leaf there was a small green parcel. The caterpillar was inside the parcel. One day, two days, three days, four days… The caterpillar was still inside the parcel.

Then one sunny day the parcel opened. What was inside? Can you guess?'

'A beautiful butterfly.'

12 They had a farm.

1 **Listen and point.** Sam's grandmother is talking about her family.

My father was a farmer. We had a little farm near Clifton. We had cows, sheep and goats. My mother had lots of chickens. I had a white pony. His name was Charlie. We didn't have a car. We had a horse and cart. We were very happy.

2 **Count the animals on the farm. Write the numbers.**

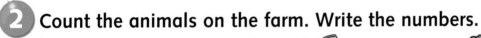

3 **Write the numbers and read.**

Grandma's family had _____ goats and _____ sheep. They had _____ cows and _____ chickens. They had _____ horse and _____ pony. They had _____ animals on the farm.

4 **What is wrong? Read and speak.**

(Grandma and Grandpa had a big farm.) (No, they had a little farm.)

They didn't have cows. Grandma's mother had ducks.

Grandma had a black pony. They didn't have a horse and cart.

1 Look, read and point.

Grandma's farm was very old. It had little windows, a big door and two tall chimneys. It had a big nest on the roof.

2 Look inside the house and find these things.

radio   lamp   rug   stove

sofa   armchair   mirror   floor   wall

3 Ask and answer.

Did they have a radio?

Yes, they did.

Did they have a TV?

No, they didn't.

Write

Write six sentences about Grandma's family.
They had ...
They did not have ...

1 **Look at this!**

past of 'have'

I	You	He
She	It	We
You	They	

+ had + noun

Did

I	you	he
she	it	we
you	they	

+ have + noun?

She had a kite.

Did she have a robot?
She did not have a robot.

Grandma had a doll. She didn't have a TV.

She didn't have a mobile phone.

My Grandma

Yes **No**

doll   kite   cat   robot   TV   mobile phone

Did she have a horse and cart?

Yes, she did.

horse and cart   ball   plane   books   train   radio   teddy

2 **Ask and answer.**

Did she have a kite?   Yes, she did.

3 **Look, listen and read.**
Grandma is going shopping. She is looking for her glasses.

Where are my glasses?

Are they in your basket?

I can't see them.

Hee! Hee! She can't see us!

Are they on the table?

I can't see them.

Hee! Hee! She can't see us!

Grandma! I can see them! They're on your head!

Hee! Hee!

1 **Look and find.**

This is Grandpa's house. Can you see …

a  garden?   a  roof?   a  swing?

a  chimney?   an  old car?

2 **Listen and ✔ the right photo.**

3 **Write.**

Write six things about Grandpa.

Grandpa had …

Granny, please comb my hair

Granny, Granny,
please comb my hair,
you always take your time,
you always take such care,

You put me on a cushion
between your knees,
you rub a little coconut oil,
parting gentle as a breeze,

Mummy, Mummy,
she's always in a hurry-hurry
rush,
She pulls my hair,
sometimes she tugs,

But Granny,
you have all the time
in the world,
and when you've finished,
you always turn my head and say,
'Now who's a nice girl!'

Grace Nichols

13 The first people were in Africa.

North America ④

1 Listen and read.

Mrs Hill is teaching the class about the first people.
Listen to the children talking about the map.

Who were the first people, Emma?

① First there were people in Africa. There was water and there were trees. There were tools*. There wasn't any fire*.

Pacific Ocean

② Next there were people in Asia. They were hunters* and they had spears*. There was fire. There weren't any houses.

③ Then there were people in Europe. It was very cold. There weren't any houses but there were caves* and warm clothes.

2 Look at the map and say.

First there were people in Africa.

There was water.

There wasn't any fire.

3 Find the * words.

Glossary

spear: This is a spear.   Hunters sometimes have spears.
tool: These are tools.   Tools are for work.
cave: This is a cave.   People can live in caves.
fire: This is a fire.   People can use fires for cooking food.
hunter: This is a hunter.   He hunts animals and eats them.

  Describing the past (history)

1 **Listen and read.**

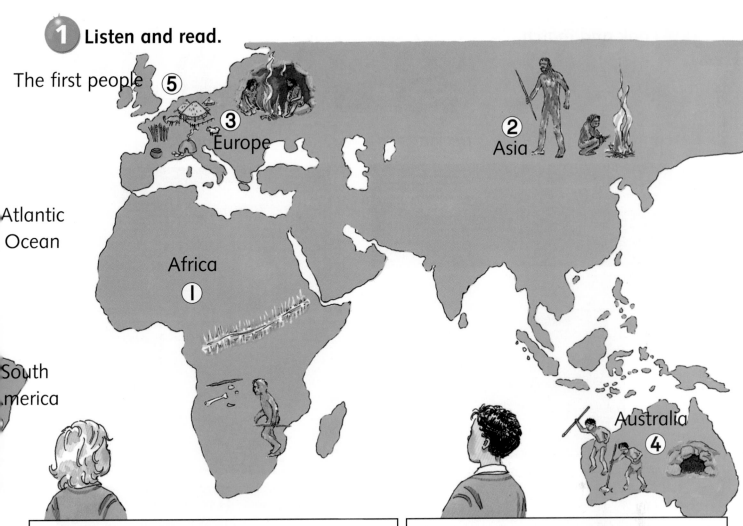

The first people ⑤

Europe ③

Asia ②

Atlantic Ocean

Africa ①

South America

Australia ④

④ Later on there were people in Australia and North and South America, too. There weren't any houses but there were caves and tents*. There were clothes and there were rings and necklaces*.

⑤ Then there were villages*. People were farmers. There were sheep and goats. There were houses and clothes and blankets*. There were pots* for food and there was bread.

2 **Find the * words.**

necklace: This is a necklace.  People wear necklaces round their necks.

pot: This is a pot. There is honey in this pot.

tent: This is a tent. People can live in tents.

blanket: This is a blanket. People put blankets on their beds.

village: This is a village.  It is smaller than a town.

Write five sentences about the first people. First ... Next...

What did the first people have?

1 **Look and match.**

 comb   knife   necklace   writing   helmet   painting

1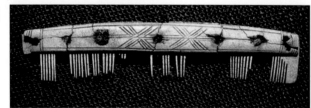

2

3

4

5

6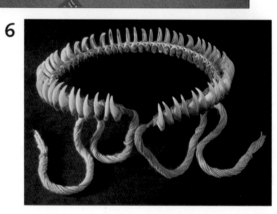

2 **Read and check. Were you right?**

I Many of the first people had combs. This comb is from Europe. It is very beautiful.

3 Some people had helmets. This helmet is from Asia. It is not heavy.

5 There was writing in Asia. Can you read this?

2 There were paintings on the walls of caves. This is a painting of a horse. It is in a cave in Europe.

4 There were knives for hunting and for eating. This knife was for eating. It is from Europe.

6 There were necklaces for men and women. This necklace is from Europe.

1 Look at this!

There was…
There were …

meat bread cheese

There was…
Was there + any …?
There was + not + any…

nuts cakes bananas

There were…
Were there + any …?
There were + not + any…

What did the first people eat?

Was there any honey?

Were there any biscuits?

Yes, there was honey.

No, there weren't any biscuits.

honey   nuts   eggs   figs   fish

meat   water   leaves   dates   grapes

2 Ask and answer.

Was there any bread?

No, there wasn't any bread.

Were there any dates?

Yes, there were dates.

3 Find, say and write.

Write about the first people. Find three things. There was... There were...

Find three things. There wasn't any... There weren't any...

Paint a pebble picture

These are cave paintings. They were on the walls of caves long ago.
You can make a pebble painting. Here is how.

Find a large pebble, a black felt-tipped pen, some paints and a paint brush.

1 Draw an animal on the pebble. Use the black felt-tipped pen.

2 Mix some red, yellow, blue and white paints with some water. Paint the animal.

You can draw these animals.

Make a necklace

The first people liked necklaces. You can make one the same. Here is how.

Find some nuts, feathers, leaves, seeds and a needle and thread.

1 Take a long thread. Sew on the nuts and seeds. Make a knot before and after.

2 Tie on the leaves and feathers.

14 You can go on rides at the funfair.

1 Match and say.

I like sea animals. Where can I learn about them?

At the aquarium.

watch puppets | read stories | watch cartoons | learn about sea animals | go on rides | look at the stars

puppet theatre | funfair | cinema

aquarium | library | science museum

2 Point, ask and answer.

Can you see Emma?

Yes, I can.

Where is she?

She's at the library.

What's she doing?

She's reading a story.

1 Listen and read.

2 Read and write the answers.

1 Why does Sam want to go to the castle? 2 Why doesn't Ned want to go to the castle? 3 Why doesn't Ned like the castle? 4 Why is Ned afraid? 5 Why isn't Sam afraid?

3 Look and say.

1 **Look at this!**

Why?
Because …

I want to go to the zoo.

Why?

Because I like animals.

I don't want to go to the cave.

Why not?

Because I'm afraid of the dark.

2 **Look and match.**

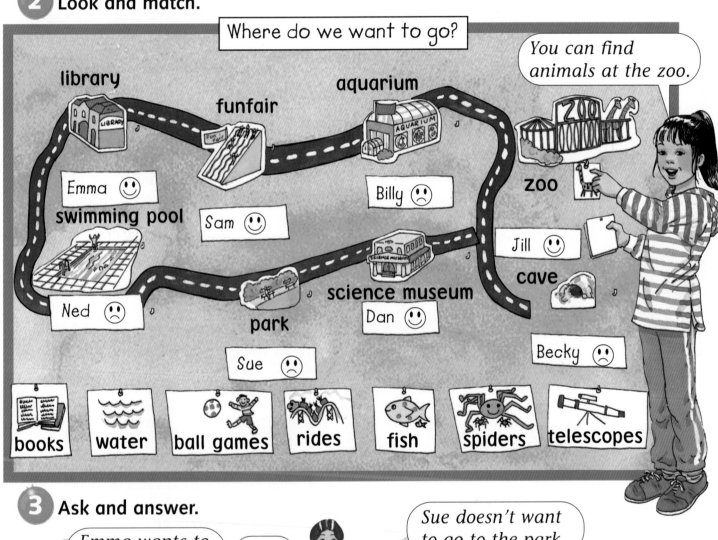

Where do we want to go?

You can find animals at the zoo.

library

funfair

aquarium

zoo

Emma ☺

swimming pool

Billy ☹

Sam ☺

Jill ☺

cave

Ned ☹

science museum

Dan ☺

park

Becky ☹

Sue ☹

books   water   ball games   rides   fish   spiders   telescopes

3 **Ask and answer.**

Emma wants to go to the library.

Why?

Because she likes books.

Sue doesn't want to go to the park.

Why not?

Because she doesn't like ball games.

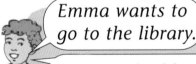

Write two sentences.
I want to … because …
I don't want to … because …

1 **Think about it.**

This is Susie. Look at the pictures. What do you think she likes? What do you think she doesn't like?

my house, my baby brother and my cat

my playhouse in the garden

my class at school and my teacher

the monkey house at the zoo

This is Mike. Look at the pictures. What do you think he likes? What do you think he doesn't like?

my friend's pony

the funfair

my father's boat on the beach

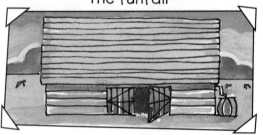

the barn on my grandfather's farm

2 **Listen and ✔.**

Susie likes her house. ____	Mike likes the pony. ____
Susie likes her playhouse. ____	Mike likes the funfair. ____
Susie likes her class. ____	Mike likes the beach. ____
Susie likes the zoo. ____	Mike likes the barn. ____

Tongue Twisters

Can you say these? ✔ if you can. Then say them faster and faster.

Red lorry, yellow lorry ☐

How much wood
would a woodchuck chuck
if a woodchuck
could chuck wood?

☐

Fuzzy Wuzzy was a bear,
A bear was Fuzzy Wuzzy.
When Fuzzy Wuzzy had no hair,
He wasn't fuzzy, was he?

☐

Peter Piper picked a peck
of pickled peppers.
A peck of pickled peppers
Peter Piper picked.
If Peter Piper picked a peck
of pickled peppers,
Where's the peck of pickled peppers
Peter Piper picked?

☐

Do you know any tongue twisters?

15 She is the prettiest.

1 Look, listen and read.

My mask is pretty.

My mask is ugly.

The children are having an art lesson. They are making masks. They are painting faces on paper plates. Some faces are pretty and some faces are ugly. Some faces are happy and some faces are sad.

Let's look at the sad masks.

My mask is sad.

My mask is sadder than yours.

Look at my mask. Mine is the saddest.

Let's look at the happy masks.

My mask is happy.

My mask is happier than yours.

Look at my mask. Mine is the happiest.

2 Ask and answer.

1  2  3   4   5   6

 Which mask is the biggest?

Number 2 is the biggest.

the smallest   the oldest   the prettiest   the youngest   the ugliest

1 Look at this!

The children are making big pictures. Can you help them?

| The green man | The blue lady | The yellow boy | The pink girl |

This is his.

2 Ask, point and answer.

Whose sock is this?

It's hers.

3 Look, point and say.

Whose is it?

It's ours!

Whose ball is it?

It's theirs.

1 Reading: Where was Jill?

Yesterday was Thursday . It was a school day. But Jill was not at school . She didn't have her school bag . It was on her bed. She didn't have her lunch box . It was on the kitchen table. She didn't have her bicycle. It was in the shed . But Jill wasn't at home. Where was she?

Jill was at the hospital ...

2 What's wrong? Read and speak.

Yesterday was Tuesday. *No, that's wrong. Yesterday was Thursday.*

Jill was at school. Jill's bag wasn't in her bedroom.

Jill was in the shed.

Jill's lunch box was in the hall. Jill had her bike.

3 Read and find.

Why was Jill at the hospital? Where was her father? Who was in the big bed? What was inside the blanket? What was he like?

Why was Jill at the hospital? She didn't have a broken leg . She wasn't ill . Her mother was there. Her father was at the hospital too. Her mother was in a big bed . There was a little bed next to her. Mother had a little yellow blanket . What was inside? It was a new baby boy ! He was fat and he had blue eyes. He didn't have any hair.

It's my new baby brother!

Write a note to Jill's teacher.
Dear Miss Hill,
Jill wasn't at school
yesterday because ...

4 Now listen.

1 Look and say. Match the letters with the pictures.

s m r f c

f p s p n

people now

the first people

2 Look and say.

The first people had fire.
There weren't any cookers.

Now there are cookers.
And we have fridges.

3 Listen and sing.

There was a tree upon a hill,
The finest tree you ever did see.
And the green grass grew all around, all around,
And the green grass grew all around.

There was branch upon a tree,
The finest branch you ever did see.
The branch was on the tree,
The tree was on the hill,
And the green grass grew all around, all around,
And the green grass grew all around.

There were some leaves upon the branch …

There was a nest upon the leaves …

There was a bird upon the nest …

There were some feathers upon the bird …

Dolphins

Dolphins live in water but they are not fish. They need air to breathe. They can stay under the water for many minutes but then they must come up to the surface. Some dolphins live in the sea; some dolphins live in rivers. They like warm water the best.

Sometimes dolphins swim close to ships. They jump out of the water again and again. They can swim very fast – up to 55 kilometres an hour. A number of dolphins swimming together is called a 'school'.

There are small dolphins and big dolphins: some are two or three metres long. Dolphins are not dangerous. They are very clever animals and they love playing. Dolphins have smiling faces. They 'speak' with high squeaks and clicking sounds.

16 The puppet theatre

1 Listen and read.

Yesterday Emma helped her mother. First she washed the dishes, next she cleaned her shoes and then she played with her brother, Joe.

THE PUPPET THEATRE
The Frog Prince
3 o'clock

I love the puppet theatre.

She walked to the supermarket and she carried home two heavy bags.

There was a poster on a wall.

Thank you, Emma. You're a good girl.

Emma's mother was very happy.

These are for you!

She had a surprise for Emma.

Two tickets for the puppet theatre! Fantastic! Can I ask Jill?

Emma looked at the tickets.

Do you want to see 'The Frog Prince' at the puppet theatre?

Then she phoned Jill.

2 Read and say.

 Emma helped her father.   *No. She helped her mother.*

First she washed the clothes.

Next she cleaned her room.

Then she played with her friend.

She walked to the library.

She carried four heavy bags.   Her mother had three tickets.   Jill phoned Emma.

Past simple   Unit 16   Lesson 1   **83**

Once upon a time there was a princess. She lived in a big castle.

I don't have any friends.

She was beautiful but she was not happy. She did not have any friends.

What's that?

One day she walked to the pond in the garden. She looked into the water.

It's an ugly frog.

Hello!

A big frog jumped out of the pond. It had a golden crown on its head. The princess did not like the frog.

I'm not an ugly frog. I'm a handsome prince. You are sad and I am sad. Together we can be happy.

The frog talked to the princess.

Please, touch my crown.

He is very handsome!

She is very beautiful!

They jumped into the water and lived happily ever after.

2 **Answer the questions.**
1 Where did the princess live?
2 Why was she sad?
3 Where did she walk?
4 What jumped out of the water?
5 What did the princess touch?
6 What did the two frogs do?

 Past simple (narrative)

1 Look at this!

past tense

I	You	He
She	It	We
You	They	

+ verb + ed

Did

I	you	he
she	it	we
you	they	

+ verb ...?

He watched TV yesterday.

Did he play football?
He did not play football.

Yesterday

watch TV | play basketball | phone a friend | walk to school | play football

Becky

Jill

Did you play basketball?

Billy

Emma

Yes, I did.

Sam

Ned

Yesterday we played football.

2 Ask and answer.

Did Becky watch TV yesterday? *Yes, she did.*

3 Now you!

Did you play basketball yesterday? *No, I didn't.*

4 Listen and read.

We walked and walked,
We talked and talked,
We laughed and laughed,
We skipped and jumped,
We hopped and hopped and hopped and hopped –
And then we stopped.

Past simple; interrogative, negative   Unit 16 Lesson 3   85

1 Listen and draw lines. Then write the numbers.

Start here:

2 Listen again. Write ✔ or ✗.

John was at the market with his mother and his sister. ☐

John's mother wanted to buy some T-shirts. ☐

John liked the singer in the market. ☐

John liked the pink flowers. ☐

The ice creams were very nice. ☐

John's mum wanted to buy fruit and vegetables. ☐

3 Write.

Write about John's morning at the market.

The three goats

Once upon a time there were three goats: a little goat, a big goat and a very, very big goat. They lived next to a river. Across the river the grass was green.

> *We're hungry. Let's go over the bridge and eat the green, green grass.*

First the smallest goat walked onto the bridge.
Under the bridge lived a small ugly man.
He jumped up onto the bridge.

> *Stop! I'm going to eat you!*

> *Please, don't! My brother's coming. He's bigger and nicer than I am.*

> *Go!*

The smallest goat walked over the bridge. Next the big goat walked onto the bridge. The small ugly man jumped up.

> *Stop! I'm going to eat you!*

> *Please, don't! My brother's coming. He's bigger and nicer than I am.*

> *Go!*

The big goat walked over the bridge. Then the biggest goat walked onto the bridge. The small ugly man jumped up.

> *Stop! I'm going to eat you!*

> *Oh no, you're not!*

The biggest goat started to run.

> *Help!*

> *BANG!*

The small ugly man went higher and higher, over the hills, over the mountains and over the rainbow.

The biggest goat walked over the bridge and into the green field. And the three goats lived happily ever after.

17 You mustn't swim after eating.

1 Listen and read.

I must do my homework first.

I must hurry. It's half past three.

See you at quarter to four!

Sam comes home at 3.00. He and Ned want to go swimming.

Sam can't go swimming now. He must do his homework.

Sam is hungry. He has a big sandwich and some chocolate cake.

Bye, Mum! I'm going swimming.

You mustn't swim after eating.

Bye!

You must have a towel!

Here comes Ned on his bike. But Sam must wait. He mustn't swim now.

Sam and Ned leave at quarter to five. Mum brings a towel.

Do you have any money? You mustn't forget your money!

Thanks, Mum.

Sorry! You must be at the pool before 5 o'clock!

Sam doesn't have any money!

Sam and Ned can't swim today. They're too late.

2 Look and say. Sam must do his homework.

3 Act out the story.

Expressing necessity

1 **Look at this!**

Do you think picture A is **must** or **mustn't**?

I think picture A is **mustn't**.

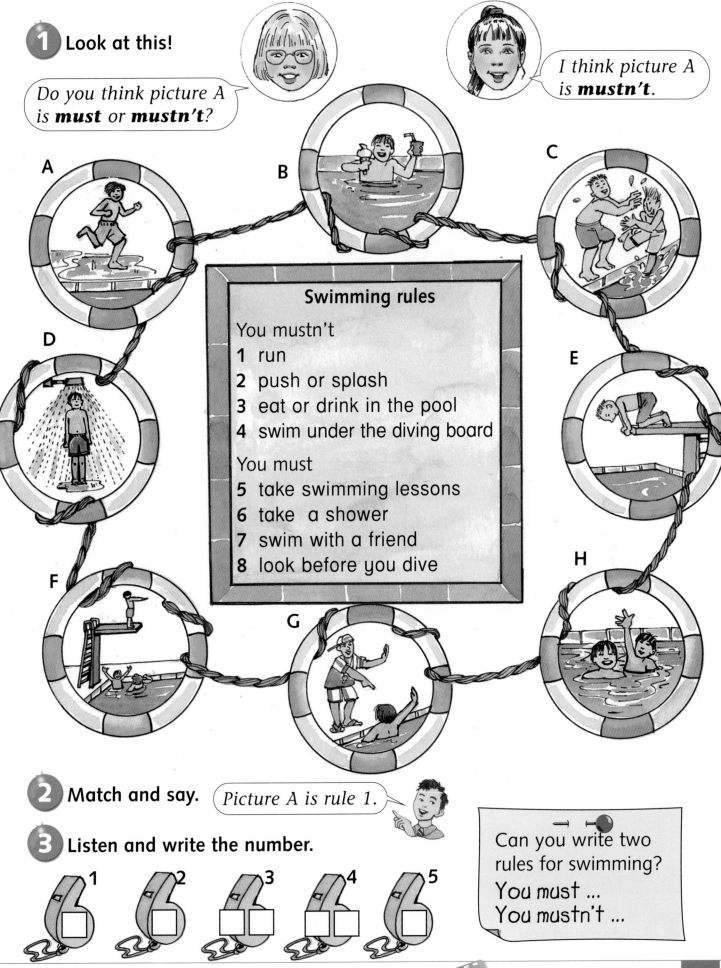

Swimming rules

You mustn't
1 run
2 push or splash
3 eat or drink in the pool
4 swim under the diving board

You must
5 take swimming lessons
6 take a shower
7 swim with a friend
8 look before you dive

2 **Match and say.** Picture A is rule 1.

3 **Listen and write the number.**

1 2 3 4 5

Can you write two rules for swimming?
You must ...
You mustn't ...

1 Read and match.

Road Safety

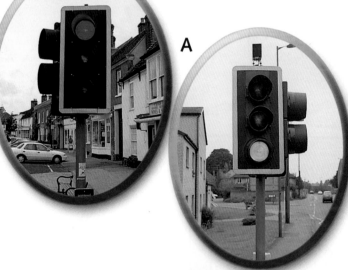

A

B

C

☐ Watch that truck, watch that truck
Rolling down the road;
It can't stop as fast as us
With its heavy load!

☐ Stop says the red light,
Go says the green,
Wait says the yellow one
Winking in between.

☐ Stop! Look! And think!
Before you cross the road.
You must use your eyes and ears
And if no car or bus appears
THEN you can cross the road.

2 Listen and say.

1 **Look at this.**

must

must +verb

must + not +verb

You must wear boots for football.

You must not wear boots for tennis.

We must wear the right clothes for sports!

cycling — Yes ✔ No ✘

skateboarding — Yes ✔ No ✘

football — Yes ✔ No ✘

swimming — swimsuit / glasses — Yes ✔ No ✘

riding — boots / shorts — Yes ✔ No ✘

tennis — socks / boots — Yes ✔ No ✘

running — Yes ✔ No ✘

watch · glasses · dress · shorts · tracksuit · socks · shoes

swimsuit · boots · trainers · helmet · kneepads

2 **Look and say.**

You mustn't wear glasses for swimming.

But you must wear a swimsuit.

3 **Listen and read.**

Billy is learning to cross the road. He is jumping up and down.
'You must stand still!' says Mum. 'Look! Can you see any cars?'

There aren't any cars. Now Billy is singing loudly.
'Be quiet!' says Mum. 'You must listen! Can you hear any cars?'

Billy hears a bicycle bell. He doesn't hear any cars. Billy looks between his legs. He sees a bicycle.
'Don't be silly!' says Mum.
'You must be careful, Mum!' says Billy.

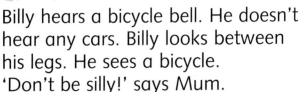

Mum moves very quickly! 'Thank you, Billy', she says.

The fox and the grapes

A fox walked under some nice grapes.
'These grapes look good,' he said.

'I want to eat them, but they're too high.
I can't reach them. I must jump for them.'
He jumped and jumped.

Again and again he jumped, but he
couldn't reach the grapes.

So he said, 'I can see them now. They're
green. They're not sweet. I don't like green
grapes. They're sour. I don't want them.'

So he walked away and he didn't have
any grapes.

The fox really wanted to eat the grapes.
Why did he say they were sour?

Because he couldn't reach them.

Don't say, 'I don't want that' just because you can't have it.

18 Seasons

January February March April May June July August September October November December

1 Read and match.

Which season is it?

A It's cold. We wear boots and gloves. There aren't any leaves. Sometimes we can ice skate.	**B** It's often warm. We can see flowers and baby animals.
C It's hot! We can wear shorts and T-shirts. We can go to the beach and we can swim.	**D** It's often cool. Some trees are brown or orange. We wear jackets.

2 Look and listen.

The children are learning about the seasons in England.

It's warm today.

It's spring. It's often warm in spring.

very hot
hot
warm
cool
cold
very cold

spring

summer

autumn

winter

3 Think about it.

Some countries have four seasons. How many seasons does your country have? Talk about the months in your country, like this:

It's often very hot in August.

Look and match.

We have a weather table. Look!

1 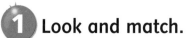   2   3   4

It's raining!   It's windy!   It's sunny!   It's snowing!

2 **Reading.**

Make a weather book for your classroom.
Find some scissors and coloured paper. Make some weather symbols:

Put them in an envelope.
Stick the envelope on a notebook.
Tie a pencil to the notebook.
Write about the weather.

Monday, 11th May

Today it is sunny and windy.
It isn't hot. It is 15 degrees.

3 **Listen, draw and match.**

What's the weather like today?

What was the weather like yesterday?

What was the weather like last winter?

What was the weather like in April?

It snowed every day.   It was very, very windy.   It's raining.   It was sunny.

1 Look at this!

rain   snow

Yesterday it rained.
Today it is raining.
Tomorrow it is going to rain.

cloudy   windy   sunny
hot   cold   cool   warm

Yesterday it was cloudy.
Today it is sunny.
Tomorrow it is going to be hot.

What was the weather like yesterday?

What's the weather like today?

What is the weather going to be like tomorrow?

Yesterday   **Today**   **Tomorrow**

cool

cold

warm

2 Ask and answer.

What was the weather like yesterday?

Yesterday it was ...

3 Play a game.

What is the weather going to be like tomorrow?

Tomorrow it's going to rain and it's going to be sunny.

Tomorrow

4 Listen and say.

Little wind

Little wind, blow on the hill-top,
Little wind, blow on the plain;
Little wind, blow up the sunshine,
Little wind, blow off the rain.

1 **Read, match and say.**

1 is picture D. There is a beach. It is hot and sunny.

1	2	3	4	5
sunny	football game	yesterday	cold	windy
beach	warm	snowed	ice	raining
hot	sunny	mountain	snowing	umbrellas
	clouds	sunny		

A

B

C

D

E

Write about two pictures.
In picture 1 there is a ...
It is ...

2 **Listen and check.**

Rain

'Splash,' said the raindrop
As it dropped on my hat.
'Splash,' said another
As it ran down my back.

'You are very rude,' I said,
As I looked up to the sky.
Then another raindrop splashed
Right in to my eye!

Clouds

White sheep, white sheep,
On a blue hill,
When the wind stops
You stand still.

When the wind blows
You walk away slow,
White sheep, white sheep,
Where do you go?

19 Read me a story, please!

1 Listen and read.

Please can I go to the park?

No, you can't.

Sam wants to play football but he can't go to the park.

I'm going shopping. You must play with Lizzie and Ben.

Hooray!

He must play with his little brother and sister.

Lizzie and Ben want a story.

Please, please, read us a story!

Once upon a time ...

Sam reads them a story.

Ben wants a picture.

Please, please, draw me a picture!

Sam draws him a picture.

Lizzie wants a song.

Please, please, sing me a song!

The wheels on the bus ...

Sam sings her a song.

Mum comes home. Where is Sam?

Hello children. Where's Sam?

Sam is sleeping.

2 Read. What is Lizzie saying?

Please!!

Read me a .

Sing me a .

Draw me a .

Give me a .

Buy me a .

Make me a .

1 Look and read.

Look at my cake.

It's good.

I think mine is better.

Mine is the best!

Ben's cake is good.   Lizzie's cake is better.   Sam's cake is the best.

2 Listen, read and write.

A   B

Sam thinks ☐ is better.

WOOF WOOF

A   B

Jill thinks ☐ is better.

A   B   C

Emma thinks ☐ is the best.

A   B   C

Ned thinks ☐ is the best.

3 Look and speak.

Which is better?

A   B

I think A is better because it's big.

A   B

Which is the best?

A   B   C

I think C is the best because it's fast.

A   B   C

1 **Look and find.**

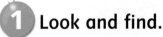

|  | | | | | |  |

brushes   a letter   a sofa   a blanket   paints   eggs   a pencil box

2 **Read and write the numbers.**

1 Danny is doing his Maths homework. Danny's mother and father are standing behind him. He is showing them his book.

2 Julie likes Art. The paints and brushes are Julie's. It is her grandmother's birthday today. Julie is painting her a picture.

3 Julie and Danny's grandmother and grandfather are going to come for dinner. Mum is making a cake.

4 Julie's baby brother is in his little bed but he cannot sleep. Julie is singing him a song.

5 Julie has a pretty picture on her desk. It was a present from her uncle. She is writing him a letter. She is saying thank you.

6 Danny is sitting on the sofa with his grandmother. She is reading him a story.

Write two things about Danny.
Write two things about Julie.

1 **Look at this!**

verb + me / him / her + noun

Sing me a song.
Write him a letter.
Tell her a story.

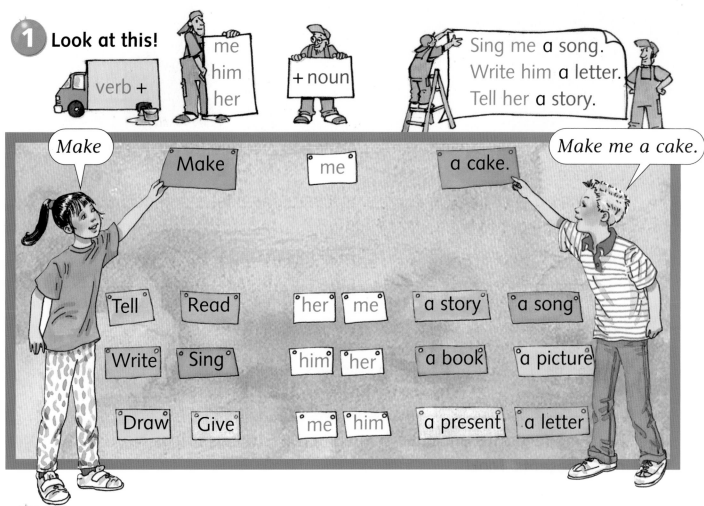

Make

Make me a cake.

Make   me   a cake.

Tell	Read	her	me	a story	a song
Write	Sing	him	her	a book	a picture
Draw	Give	me	him	a present	a letter

2 **Now you!**

3 **Listen and read.**

Ice is nice,
Ice cream is better,
Bananas and cream are the best.

Bananas and cream,
Bananas and cream,
Bananas and cream are the best.

What do we dream about?
What do we scream about?
Ice is nice
And ice cream is better –
But bananas and cream are the best, the best,
Yes, bananas and cream are the best.

Uncle Fred

My Uncle Fred is a pilot. He flies planes to America, to Australia and to Africa.

He wears a dark blue jacket and trousers and a blue and gold cap. He is very handsome!

We do not see him very often but he always sends us postcards.

He is my favourite uncle. He is the best! He always brings me nice presents. Look!

A necklace from India.   A dress from England.   A drum from Africa.

A bear from Australia.   A money box from Egypt.   A mask from America.
Last week he was in China. This is his present from China.

Grrr!

What do you think it is?

20 See what I can do ...

1 Read and write.

Ten things about me!

1 My name is _____ .

2 I go to _____ school.

3 I live in _____ .

4 I am _____ years old.

5 My birthday is on _____ .

6 I am _____ centimetres tall.

7 My eyes are _____and my hair is _____ .

8 My favourite toy is _____ .

9 I like eating _____ .

10 My favourite sport is _____ .

2 Play a game: Word Beetles

How many legs does your beetle have?

Mine has five legs. How many does yours have?

1 **What are they saying? Write A for** Yes, you can. **or B for** No, you can't.

2 **Look and say.**

Look at the pictures. How are the pictures different? Use these words.

| heavy | light | tall | short | long | pretty | ugly | old | young | happy | sad |

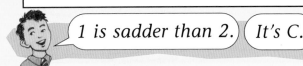 1 is sadder than 2. It's C.

 3 is the lightest. It's F.

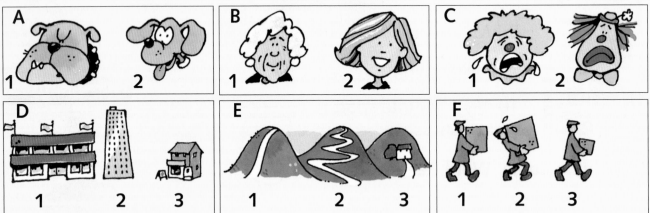

3 **Play a game: The fantastic dinner.**

I'd like some ice cream, please.

I'd like some ice cream and some bread, please.

I'd like some ice cream, some bread and an apple, please.

  I'd like ...

1 **A quiz. Read and find.**

1 Who plays the guitar?
2 Whose father has a boat?
3 Who has a little brother called Joe?
4 Who lives in a flat over a corner shop?
5 Who lives near the sea?

6 What is this seagull called?

7 Where did this girl live?

8 Why was this girl at the hospital?

9 What did this fox want?

10 Why was this girl sad?

11 Why doesn't this boy want to go to the castle?

12 What does this woman do?

13 Where are these girls going to go?

14 Why can't this boy play football in the park?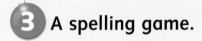

15 What did this dog do?

2 **Listen and check.**

3 **A spelling game.**

c   a   s   t   l   e

Can you spell castle?

That's right. 2 points.

1 **Find and say.**

Look through your book!

 Which boy or girl do you like best? Why?

 Which story do you like best? Can you talk about it?

Which is your favourite song? Can you sing it?

 Which is your favourite poem? Can you say it?

2 **Write.**

 Can you write three things about your book?

I like ... because ...

3 **Listen and sing.**

The train is coming, oh yeah.
The train is coming, oh yeah.
The train is coming,
The train is coming,
The train is coming, oh yeah.

Go and get the tickets, oh yeah.

The train is leaving, oh yeah.

We're going through the tunnel, oh yeah.

We're going through the city, oh yeah.

We're stopping at the station, oh yeah.

Bedtime

Five minutes, five minutes more, please!

Let me stay five minutes more!

Can't I just finish the castle

I'm building here on the floor?

Can't I just finish this bead-chain –

It almost is finished, look!

Can't I just finish this game, please?

When a game's once begun

It's a pity never to find out

Whether you've lost or won.

Can't I just stay five minutes?

Well, can't I stay just four?

Three minutes, then? Two minutes?

Can't I stay one minute more?

Eleanor Farjeon

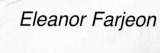

seagull

caterpillar

feather

nuts

bicycle

branch

grass

carpenter

plumber

sailor

train driver

pilot

cook

farmer

spaceman

teacher

reporter

artist

HOSPITAL

POLICE

DENTIST

AMBULANCE

Cafe

BAKERY

FRUIT AND VEGETABLES

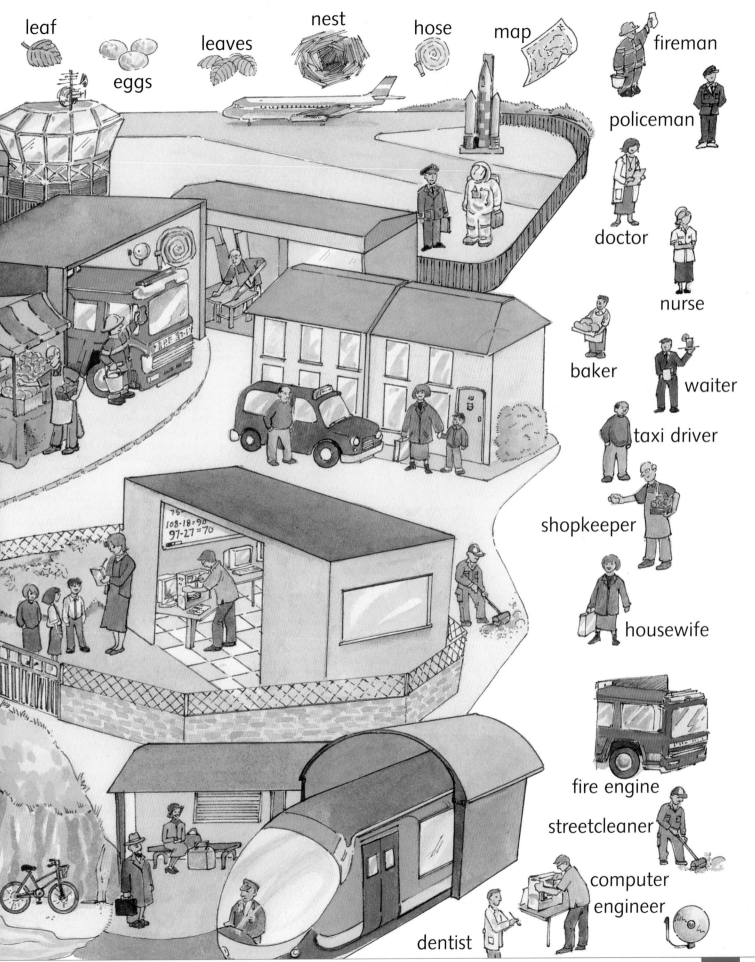

leaf

eggs

leaves

nest

hose

map

fireman

policeman

doctor

nurse

baker

waiter

taxi driver

shopkeeper

housewife

fire engine

streetcleaner

computer engineer

dentist

camera

necklace

jeans

pullover

trainers

blanket

towel

cloud

waterfall

pool

rock

cave

lighthouse

radio

lettuce

sandwich

tomatoes

mug

cheese

picnic

plate

knife

fork

bowl

bread

orange juice

icebox